IT CAME
FROM
OHIO...

Also by James Renner:

Nonfiction
The Serial Killer's Apprentice
Amy: My Search for Her Killer

Fiction
The Man from Primrose Lane

IT CAME FROM OHIO...

TRUE TALES OF THE WEIRD, WILD, AND UNEXPLAINED

JAMES RENNER

ILLUSTRATIONS BY TODD JAKUBISIN

GRAY & COMPANY, PUBLISHERS
CLEVELAND

For Toby

Gray & Company, Publishers
www.grayco.com

ISBN: 978-1-59851-063-8
Printed in the United States of America
v1

CONTENTS

FOREWORD

IN THE DARKNESS, WE BELIEVE

Inevitably, the question is asked in every lasting relationship. After you've talked of siblings and first loves, your favorite music and your favorite color, and it has grown dark outside and the lights have dimmed, and it's just you alone with another human being, listening to the fulcrums of each other's life journeys, the question is posed: "What is the strangest thing that has ever happened to you?"

Sometimes, it's phrased a little differently: "What's the scariest thing that's ever happened to you?" or "Do ya have any weird stories?"

The one I ask of my new friends as a sort of litmus test to calculate my further interest in them, for I believe interesting people are byproducts of a few random extraordinary events, is this: "Has anything ever happened to you that you cannot explain logically?"

I have never been disappointed by the answer.

The most straight-edged skeptic will still have a nugget of a story that, on the surface, defies explanation. And everyone, when recalling this memory they keep locked in a room in the farthest recesses of their mind, takes on the same reverent tone when dispensing these odd truths. Because, in those stories, we get a glimpse at something *more*, don't we? Something beyond the limits and confines of logical reality. Something bigger. A sense of the paranormal, of spirits, of creatures lurking in the shadows, of our oldest nightmares made real.

My grandfather, who served in the Pacific theater in WWII, sometimes spoke of giant snakes—big enough to eat men—that lived in the jungles of Fiji. He spoke of the way the undersides of navy vessels glowed at night with phantom light.

Two years after I first met my buddy Charles, I asked him The Question, and he told me a story about running through downtown Cleveland one afternoon and seeing a boy dressed in Depression-era clothing dart from behind a building and then disappear before his eyes, like a vapor.

I have spoken to FBI agents who hear dark voices at the site where Amy Mihaljevic's body was recovered.

My aunt tells the story—I kid you not—of seeing the Easter bunny in the furry flesh as a child. She has become convinced over the years that what she actually saw was an angel pretending to be the Easter bunny to please her child mind. I like that explanation, actually.

I have collected a handful of strange stories of my own. I suppose it's a byproduct of my profession, reporting. Journalism opens doors for me that are shut for most people. For instance, I've spent a night inside the Mansfield reformatory (avoid the showers). I've tracked a suspected murderer to Key West, Florida, who seemed enveloped in a visible darkness (Yes, I know how that sounds). I once watched a row of strange aircraft disappear over Portage County (My father, who was with me that day, owns that story and tells it at every opportunity).

But nothing quite comes close to the weirdness I experienced one particular evening at Camp Manatoc, when I was fourteen years old.

It was twilight and I was with my best friend, Toby Pease, the senior patrol leader of Troop 558 (and now an analyst for the Federal Reserve). We were setting up a tent on a grassy hill when we saw the end of the world crashing through the sky. It was a bright green ball of light, trailing silent fire across the heavens. A meteor, obviously. But it was damn close. Too close. And too big.

"Oh, that's not good," said Toby, in his droll way. I think we both suspected it would be his last words.

We watched the ball of fire disappear behind the treetops and braced for the shockwave that would signal its impact. But it never came. Not even a sound.

"Let's go see," I suggested.

And so Toby and I set off into the woods, the deep

dark woods of the Cuyahoga Valley National Park system. Deep and old and hungry woods.

The sun was setting and the light was leaving the world but we made our way quickly over several ravines, marching in the direction of where the meteor (or whatever it was—by then we were already wondering if it might have been a flying saucer, you know, like the one at Roswell) crashed.

Toby saw them first. "What the hell?"

I felt something dripping on my neck. It felt like rain but it wasn't raining.

I followed Toby's gaze toward the trunk of a large oak tree. The tree seemed to be moving, undulating.

Something was covering the giant tree. We stepped closer.

Millions. *Billions* of little creatures covered the trunk and scuttled slowly up the branches above. They looked like tufts of cotton. I realized with horror that what was dripping on my neck was their excrement.

You can imagine how quickly we departed the area. We were convinced that some extraterrestrial bug had come down on the meteor or spaceship or whatever had crashed and was now multiplying, beginning to eat our planet whole.

In hindsight, the creatures were probably aphids and had nothing to do with the meteor. Certainly, they have not yet taken over Camp Manatoc, let alone the world.

And still . . .

Sometimes, in the quiet hours after midnight, I lie awake and wonder. What did we really see that night as teenagers? After all, as you'll discover in this book, Camp Manatoc is no stranger to scary stories. Some people think reality is stretched thin, there.

During the day, in the light, we can afford to be logical.

But in the darkness, we know better.

In the darkness, we believe.

So turn on a night light, lock your door (dead bolt, just in case), and close the window blinds, because I want to tell you some more stories. I can't say they're true. Not for sure.

Let that be some comfort to you until the light returns.

COPS AND ALIENS

THE FLYING SAUCER NAMED FLOYD AND THE MANY LIVES IT RUINED

The last contact Dale Spaur had with the media was in October 1966, a few months after "The Incident." A reporter named John de Groot found him living out of a motel room in Solon, barely surviving on $80 a week— living off bowls of cereal and the occasional sandwich. He looked sickly, a shell of a man. Spaur said it had found him again, the flying saucer he'd chased into Pennsylvania earlier that year, when he was still a respected sheriff's deputy with a family. He called the flying saucer "Floyd," his middle name.

And then, like the UFO, Spaur disappeared.

For forty years, the public was left wondering how the story ended and what had become of Dale Spaur.

Then, in 2006, quite out of the blue, Spaur's son contacted me and hinted at a more sinister ending, the kind Stephen King might have written for the guy.

We met at a greasy spoon in Kent—Mike's Place, the joint with the X-wing fighter parked out front. The first thing you should know about James, Dale Spaur's son, is that he's a giant, a large imposing man, just like his father, who was six-feet-four-inches. The type of fellow who usually isn't afraid of anything.

"I'm his flesh and blood," said James. "But there was a part of him that was always hidden. He wouldn't even tell me everything."

What he did tell him, though, was enough to make his skin crawl.

And it all began that far-away night in 1966, along a desolate stretch of road in southern Portage County, when his father and another deputy came across that abandoned '59 Ford full of strange electronic equipment . . .

The following description of events is taken from actual documented interviews, police reports, and military memos written in the weeks following the unexplained events of April 17, 1966.

Dale Spaur's shift began promptly at midnight. He was on patrol that morning with Deputy Wilbur Neff, cruising the dusty roads of Portage County. The early hours of April 17 were routine, at least at first. They visited the site of a car crash and sent the driver to the hospital and waited for a tow. They stopped for coffee. Around 5:07 a.m. Spaur and Neff were in route to a nearby hospital when they passed an abandoned car on the side of State Route 224, east of Randolph.

The rusty vehicle was parked at the edge of a nest of dark woods. The driver was nowhere to be seen. They parked the cruiser. Spaur stepped over to the vehicle while Neff remained by their patrol car. So it was Spaur who saw the strange design on the side of the abandoned car. It was a triangle with a lightning bolt inside. "Seven Steps to Hell" was written above it. Inside the car was a bunch of electronic equipment and old radios.

Suddenly, Spaur caught site of a light in the sky to the south. As he turned to it, he realized it was close. Very close. It was some kind of craft, large and oval. It hovered just above the treetops, about 500 feet above their heads. It emitted a brilliant blue-white spotlight that shot down straight below it. The light hit the cruiser. Suddenly, the road, the woods, and the car were bathed in light "as bright as daylight." As it moved, the saucer slowly tipped forward as if pulled by some invisible force. It made no noise other than a faint humming. Spaur later explained that it actually

A half hour before Dale Spaur spotted the UFO, it was seen over downtown Mantua. Police Chief Gerald Buchert managed to snap off a few grainy photographs of the saucer, hovering over street lights, before it disappeared. The photos can still be found at the police station, where his son, Harry, is now chief.

sounded like "a whisper behind a humming." As he ran back to the cruiser, Spaur had the sensation that reality was warping and that the patrol car might disappear if he touched it. That didn't happen.

Once they were inside, Spaur radioed back to base. The saucer settled gently over them, as if waiting to see what they would do next.

"P-13 to base," said Spaur. Deputy Robert Wilson answered and listened as Spaur updated him on the strange situation unfolding out on Route 224. "It's about fifty feet across, and I can just make out a dome or something on top, but that's very dark. The bottom is real bright . . . It's like it's *sitting* on the beam." The cruiser's headlights, he noted, were overpowered by the saucer's light.

"Dale," said Wilson, "do you have your .44 Magnum with you?"

"I do."

"Take a shot at it."

"I don't think I want to do that. Listen, Bob. This

If you plot Spaur's pursuit of the saucer in a map and continue further east beyond the point where he lost track of the object, you will come to the small town of Kecksburg, Pennsylvania, where residents claim a flying saucer crashed landed on December 9, 1965.

thing's a monster! It's like looking down the middle of hell."

A moment later, Wilson came back with new orders: stay put and wait for the camera car being sent from headquarters.

But then the saucer pitched forward and started off east, over 224. Spaur and Neff followed. It began to accelerate. Spaur kept pace. Soon they were traveling at speeds in excess of 100 miles per hour down State Route 14, through the sleepy hamlets of Deerfield and North Benton. If the saucer was trying to elude the police, it had picked the wrong deputy—Spaur was a former stock car racer.

As dawn broke on the horizon, the craft was silhouetted and Spaur and Neff could make out an antenna or "probe," about twenty feet long, sticking out of the back of the saucer.

The chase continued.

As the saucer, with the deputies in hot pursuit, shot through his jurisdiction at a little over eighty-five miles an hour, East Palestine patrolman Wayne Huston joined the chase. He later described the object as "a flattened ice cream cone" zooming across the sky.

Nearing the Pennsylvania border, Spaur radioed back to Wilson and asked him to call in the cavalry. Wilson phoned Youngstown Air Force Base and told them to get a bird in the sky after it.

A few miles across the state line, Spaur's cruiser began to sputter. They were low on gas. He drove toward an Atlantic gas station just outside Freedom, on Route 65. A patrolman from Conway, Pennsylvania, named Frank Panzanella pulled into the station, just ahead of them.

"Did you see it?" Spaur asked as he, Neff, and Huston jumped out of their vehicles.

Of course Panzanella had seen it. In fact, he had been following it, too. He described it later as "a football cut in half along its length."

A moment later, as the four lawmen watched, the object accelerated upward and disappeared into the darkness of space.

Disappointed, but still excited from the adrenalin of the chase, Spaur gassed up the cruiser and began the seventy-three-mile trip back to Ravenna. He and Neff were unprepared for what awaited them back home.

News of the chase had reached the media. The station was being flooded with phone calls from reporters from all over the country. A Civil Defense official was there, too. He wanted to check the deputies for exposure to radiation, but a Geiger counter picked up nothing unusual.

The next day, the military dispatched Major Hector

Project Blue Book Director Hector Quintanilla's son, Karl, is a believer in UFOs and has worked on several saucer documentaries for SyFy.

Quintanilla, Jr., to the scene. Quintanilla was the director of Project Blue Book, our government's official UFO investigatory division, which was based out of Wright-Patterson Air Force Base in Dayton. His first words to Spaur were, "Tell me about this mirage you saw."

Four days later, Quintanilla released the military's official report on the Portage County UFO chase: Spaur and Neff had first observed "an Echo satellite" and had then pursued the planet Venus all the way into Pennsylvania. It had all been an illusion, said Quintanilla.

For Spaur, the mocking newspaper headlines that followed were not his biggest concern. Quintanilla's report had called his judgment into question. He worried what a defense attorney would do to him on the stand the next time he had to testify about something as mundane as a speeding ticket. After all, he was now known as the man who had chased Venus into Pennsylvania.

The stress of it all became too much for Spaur. He began to disappear for days at a time. One night, a couple months after the sighting, he flew into a rage at home. He grabbed his wife and shook her, hard. He was thrown in jail on a domestic violence charge. When he got out, he turned in his badge, signed divorce papers, and left town.

By the time reporter John de Groot caught up with him in October, for a follow-up story on the UFO, Spaur was living out of a seedy motel. He had lost a lot of weight and had taken to calling the flying saucer "Floyd," his middle name. It was following him, he told de Groot. Floyd was not done with him yet.

For many years, Spaur's ultimate fate was a mystery.

*   *   *

James was playing in the yard when his father finally returned to Portage County.

"This yellow-and-white four-wheel Chevy truck pulls into the driveway," he recalls. "When the driver stepped out it was like he never stopped unfolding. He was huge. 'Are you really my dad?' I asked. 'Yes, Jimmy, I'm your dad,' he said."

A few years later, James moved in with his father and his stepmother at their new house in Rocky River. This was the late '70s, and Spaur was managing the Avenue bar in Lakewood. Occasionally, he asked his father about the UFO named Floyd, but Spaur didn't like to talk about it. Eventually, he managed to pry

Stephen Spielberg was inspired by Dale Spaur's account of the flying saucer. When he got around to making *Close Encounters of the Third Kind*, he started the film with an homage to Spaur; a cop car chasing a UFO across Ohio.

some information about his father's missing years from relatives.

According to family members, after leaving the motel, Spaur moved to Amsted, West Virginia, where he worked for a taxi service for a while. On a hike in the woods one day, Spaur fell into an abandoned mine shaft. He was rushed to a hospital, but his prognosis was not good. He slipped into a coma.

"He would lie there, asleep, with his eyes open," says James. "There was a nurse there who would sit with him sometimes. But one day, she comes running out of his room, screaming. She refused to ever go in his room again. When the family asked her why, she told them that he was an alien. That my dad's body was possessed by an alien."

The nurse never knew about Spaur's famous car chase—he couldn't have told her, after all, as he was comatose by the time he arrived at the hospital.

Then, one day, Spaur just woke up. It was a miraculous recovery. When he regained his strength, he returned to Ohio, where he lived out the remainder of his life entertaining Lakewood barflies.

Spaur died in 1983. James was there. And so were a group of Inuit Indians nobody remembers inviting.

To this day, Spaur's encounter remains one of the most credible UFO sightings in history.

A BIG, FAT, HAIRY DEAL

DID A WEREWOLF TERRORIZE A SMALL OHIO TOWN IN 1972?

Defiance, Ohio, as its name suggests, had a rather auspicious beginning. The town sits by the old site of Fort Defiance, at the confluence of the Maumee and Auglaize Rivers, in northwest Ohio. Back in 1794, the western fort was overseen by General Anthony Wayne, known lovingly as "Mad Tony" to his troops. Anyhow, it was this General Wayne who, with much hubris, christened the place thus: "I *defy* the English, Indians, and all the devils of hell to take it!" They would come to learn that it's not wise to tease the devils of hell, for they might just decide to visit.

The first time he saw the monster, Ted Davis was attaching an air hose between two cars at the Norfolk & Western rail yards off Fifth Street. He and Tom Jones worked the graveyard shift for the N&W. It was about

4 a.m. on July 25, 1972, and the moon was out. Suddenly, he realized they were not alone.

"I saw these two hairy feet," he later told the Toledo *Blade*. "Then I looked up and he was standing there with that big stick over his shoulder. When I started to say something, he took off for the woods."

It was no wayward hobo, hoping to ride the rails. "It had huge, hairy feet, fangs, and it ran side-to-side like a caveman in the movies."

Less than a week later, the town grocer was accosted by the beast. It came upon him in the dark and smacked him, hard, with a two-by-four, then ran away. The grocer swore it was no normal man. It was hairy, with "some kind of animal head."

That same night, Davis saw it at the rail yard again, peering out at him from the edge of the woods.

Then the editor of the local paper, Ellen Armstrong, caught wind of the werewolf sightings and all hell broke loose. "Horror Movie Now Playing on Fifth Street," was the headline of her first story. The paper had fun with the police reports, beginning the article

The Ancient Indian tribe of the Miami once lived in the area now known as Defiance. They believed a shape-shifter god named Wisakatchekwa lived near the river and liked to tease people who came by.

with this spooky poem, from the 1941 Lon Chaney creature-feature classic *The Wolf Man*:

"Even a man who is pure of heart,

And says his prayers by night,

May become a wolf when the wolfbane blooms,

And the moon is clear and bright."

"Wolfman Reports Persist," ran the headline in *The Crescent-News* the next day. Residents were beginning to panic. "Three persons, near hysteria, sought police protection from 'the thing,' although they never saw it. At 1:24 a.m. today a man came into the police station to report that something had followed him on foot from Deatrick and S. Clinton Street to the Hotel Henry. He indicated he didn't see anything but knew it was there because he had 'a crawly feeling up the back of his neck.' The report said the man was near hysteria and spent the remainder of the night in the lobby of the hotel."

That night, a woman called the police to say she could hear something scratching at her front door and that "if anything comes through, I will shoot it!"

On May 27, 2011, a twenty-year-old man was arrested in Lorain, Ohio, after he began to growl at police. He told them he was about to become a werewolf. He was charged with underage drinking.

Chief of Police Donald Beckler had heard enough. He appealed to the Toledo *Blade* to get the word out about the spate of assaults in his small town. If it was just a kid in a mask, scaring people, it wasn't funny anymore. Someone was likely to be hurt. "We don't think it's a prank," he told the *Blade*. "He's coming at people with a club in his hand. We think it's to the safety of our people to be concerned."

And just as quickly as the attacks began, they stopped. Perhaps it was just a kid in a mask who'd taken a joke one step too far. Perhaps it was just a hairy hobo, riding the rails.

But perhaps it really was a modern-day wolfman. Perhaps the poor shifting soul saw the chief's quote in the morning paper and recognized it as a declaration of war. Perhaps the wolfman left for more remote areas of middle Ohio, those tracts of flat land between towns, where people live off-the-grid in clapboard shacks, where those who vanish have no one to report them missing . . .

Two twelve-year-olds in Niles, Ohio, reported a close encounter with a werewolf there, and claimed they'd seen it living out of a cave in the woods.

THE BALLAD OF THE LOVELAND FROG

AN INDIAN LEGEND STILL HAUNTS THE LITTLE MIAMI RIVER

A knock on the door. That's how most stories begin. Because most stories are about the search for truth, in one way or another. And secrets are hidden behind locked doors. Only an invitation can bring you inside.

On this day, I've traveled across Ohio to the bucolic town of Loveland, a suburb of Cincinnati located on the hills that roll beside the Little Miami River. It's the beginning of spring, and the sound of the peepers carries through the town. I'm on a side street lined with humble one-story homes with well-kept lawns. I'm looking for a man named Ray Shockey, a former police officer. I want to ask him about a particular night in 1972 and what he saw back then. So I knock on the door.

An elderly woman appears on the threshold. You can tell she's used to frequent visitors in the way grandmas are. "Yes?"

"Is Ray Shockey here?"

"Which one?" Apparently Ray, Sr., was somewhere inside.

"The one that saw the thing. The . . . frogman?"

"Oh, Lord. That was my son. But he doesn't like to talk about it."

"Why not?"

"Some people made fun of him about it." She grows silent for a beat, as if she's debating whether or not to say more. Finally, she says, "I was here that night. He came over after it happened. He was scared to death. Said, 'Ma, you're not gonna believe what I just saw.'" She lowers her voice a bit, then, for what she has to say next. "He shot at it, you know."

*   *   *

The first modern day sighting of what has come to be called "the Loveland Frog," was in 1955, seventeen years before Shockey's encounter. A businessman, on his way through Loveland at about 3 a.m. on May 25, spotted three figures sitting on the river bridge. He described them as humanoid, with wrinkles instead of hair, and big gaping mouths like a frog's. One held some sort of device in its hand, wand-like, that emitted blue sparks. The air around the creatures smelled strongly of alfalfa and almonds. Needless to say, the wayward businessman did not stick around.

On March 3, 1972, during a late-night patrol, Shockey noticed something lying on the ground as his cruiser approached Twightwee Road. At first, he thought it was a dog (sick or dead, perhaps). But suddenly the thing leapt up and bounded across the road in front of his headlights. According to later reports, Shockey described the monster as being about three to five feet tall, with matted hair and leathery skin and a distinct froglike face. Later, Shockey would return with another police officer in an attempt to corroborate his sighting. All that was left, though, were several long "scrape" marks leading down to the river.

A couple weeks later, Shockey's partner, Mark Matthews, pulled over for what he, too, mistook for an injured animal lying on the side of the road by the river. But when he stopped the car, the thing stood up and slowly stepped over the side of the guardrail, keeping its eyes on the policeman, before running down to the water. Matthews drew his sidearm and got off

The classic horror flick _The Creature from the Black Lagoon_ premiered in 1954, and many reporters believed the man who reported the 1955 sighting had probably seen the movie one too many times.

a shot, but not quickly enough. His initial description matched what Shockey had seen earlier that month

Loveland is a small, somewhat isolated community, a place where strange stories spread as quickly as the flu. Soon, just about everybody had heard about the two policemen who'd seen a monster out on Twight-wee Road. It was a funny story. Unless you were the two policeman. For them, the notoriety was more than embarrassing. How do you command respect when you believe a frog monster is living in the local river?

Soon enough, Shockey and Matthews would no longer talk about it, except for maybe with each other. Matthews got so frustrated with the legend he changed his story when contacted by a reporter with *X Project Magazine*, in 2001. "It was and is no 'monster'," he claimed. "It was not three to five feet tall. It did not stand erect. The animal I saw was obviously some type of lizard that someone had as a pet that either got too large for its aquarium, escaped by accident or they simply got tired of it. It was less than three feet in length, ran across the road and was probably blinded by my headlights. It presented no aggressive action."

But if that's all it was, why did he shoot at it?

*   *   *

I found Ray Shockey, Jr., at his home, not far from his parents' place. He's a big, muscular fellow with a white goatee and an affable smile. Welcoming, but short on words.

"I made up my mind a long time ago, never to talk about it again," he says. "It gave me so much grief."

In fact, the only time he's spoken about the Loveland Frog in recent years was during a conversation with the town council. He tried to convince them to market the monster a bit, put the image on town signs as a way to draw in tourists. But apparently, the town elders don't yet see the value of a good legend.

As I turn back to the car, he stops me.

"I will tell you this much," he says. "It wasn't a frog. Wasn't an iguana, either."

"What was it?"

"It was . . . bigger."

*   *   *

Turns out the legend is older than anyone suspected. *Much* older. Even Shockey didn't know about the first recorded sighting of the Loveland Frog, which occurred before the town of Loveland was even constructed.

The exact dates are kind of sketchy, but sometime around 1696, a group of French missionaries befriended a tribe of Indians who lived along the wide

Sightings of frogmen have been reported along the riverbanks of Bishopville, South Carolina, and Milton, Kentucky, too.

muddy rivers in what is now southwestern Ohio. This tribe was believed to be part of the Miami culture, but were known as the Twightwee by the Delaware people. The Twightwees warned the Frenchmen about the river demon that lived in the Little Miami. They called it the Shawnahooc.

The Shawnahooc was a human-like creature with no nose and wrinkled skin. A Twightwee hunting party had once spotted the Shawnahooc while returning to their village. One warrior shot an arrow at it. But the Shawnahooc only jumped back into the river and disappeared. They believed the Shawnahooc could never be killed.

But the story of the Shawnahooc was forgotten long ago. Even the legend of the Loveland Frog has faded in time. Inside Paxton's Grill, named for the first white settler (a man who ate Christmas dinner with George Washington at Valley Forge), the only person who recalls the story is the bartender. And he has his own suspicions.

"I think if you drink enough and you sit down by that river, you see just about everything," he says.

The bartender would rather talk about the other

The legend of the Loveland Frog is featured prominently in the author's first novel, _The Man from Primrose Lane._

oddity of Loveland, a large castle built by a Boy Scout leader on land he got free for buying a subscription to the *Cincinnati Enquirer* in the 1920s. The castle is haunted, you see. But that's a story for another day.

THE MOTHMAN COMETH

ITS FIRST VICTIM WAS FROM OHIO

This steak house is out of some David Lynch movie, this one-room greasy spoon decorated with posters of monsters drawn by child's hands. See it well. The walls are painted a garish orange that does not exist in nature. Old timers in a booth near the back chain smoke cigarettes—still legal in restaurants in West Virginia. The menu is full of meat. For about eight dollars you can get the Mothman burger, a charbroiled patty covered in pepperjack and Mothman sauce, whatever that might be. Everything is Mothman here.

The Harris Steak House is one of the few businesses that has eked out a living on Main Street. Before the Silver Bridge collapsed into the Ohio River in 1967, taking forty-six souls with it and ending a string of monster sightings, this was the center of a thriving town. Today, it's a row of empty store fronts.

The cook, a soft-spoken woman named Hazel De-Witt, saunters over with a plate of meatloaf for the reporter and a sandwich for herself.

"My brother and sister saw it," she says. "Out by the fairground, by TNT. Six feet tall. Grayish white. Wings with feathers. Lots of people think it has wings like a moth but it has wings with feathers. It landed on the hood of their car and stared at them with blood-red eyes, round and slanting like moths' eyes."

*   *   *

The Mothman has been adopted by Point Pleasant, West Virginia, as their official monster—but it all began in Salem, Ohio, on November 14, 1966.

According to published newspaper accounts, Newell Partridge was at home in Salem that night, watching television with his dog, Bandit, at his side. Suddenly, the TV started making strange noises, pulsing like a generator. Bandit barked loudly and appeared agitated. When the dog started to howl, Partridge grabbed a flashlight and took Bandit out to find what was upsetting the animal and the TV.

Mothmen have been spotted across the U.S. throughout history. Ancient Americans speak of a great thunderbird. And in 1880, several witnesses spotted a winged man flying over Coney Island.

There was something in Partridge's field—two red lights, like large traffic reflectors, staring back at them. Whatever it was, it was too far to make out any shape. Bandit took off into the field. Partridge called after his dog, but it never returned. And the lights soon vanished.

Partridge found the dog miles away, on the side of the road, its body drained of blood.

The very next evening, just 100 miles south, in Point Pleasant, two young couples cruising the back roads in a car spotted a dead dog on the side of the road, near the area of town known as TNT, which had once been used by the military but was abandoned—neighborhood kids used it as a place to make out and smoke reefer. A short way past the dead dog, the teens spotted a terrifying creature standing in a field. It was seven feet tall and stood like a man. Folded behind its torso were great wings like a bat's. When it leaped into the air, the boy behind the wheel took off, and even though he accelerated to speeds over 100 miles an hour, they all later claimed the Mothman was able to keep pace for a while. Its wings, they said, sounded like a record player on its highest setting when they beat back and forth.

"But it was those eyes that got us. It had two big eyes like automobile reflectors," added Linda Scarberry, one of the girls in the car that night.

Wherever the creature came from, it seemed to settle in the region around Point Pleasant, West Virginia, and Gallipolis, Ohio, the town just across the river. Over the course of the next year, over a hundred people reported sightings to the police. Several more reported missing dogs. Some residents believed the thing was an oversized heron known in those parts as a "shitepoke," or possibly a big owl. Others say the Mothman was an ancient harbinger of doom, the kind seen by prophets in the Old Testament. And they may be on to something because the sightings stopped on December 15, 1967, a tragic and historic day for the two towns that straddled the Ohio River.

It happened during rush hour. The Silver Bridge was packed with cars carrying families on their way home after work. Just after 5 p.m., a single eye bolt on top of the suspension bridge, damaged during manufacture, failed. The load mass shifted to a partner bolt, but it was too much weight. The bridge fell like a house of cards. Vehicles disappeared into the cold river below. Forty-six people died that day. Two bodies were never found. And the Mothman was never seen again.

*   *   *

Was 1966 the most frightening year in which to live in Ohio? Seven months before the Mothman ate Newell Partridge's dog, Portage County deputies encountered a UFO in Portage County. Could the two strange tales be connected?

Today, a fellow named Jeff Wamsley operates a Mothman museum just down the street from the Harris Steak House. Inside, you'll find a giant room full of monster memorabilia as well as a complete collection of original newspaper articles for those hoping to do a little research. There are Mothman tours. There's also stuff like t-shirts and bumper stickers and a viewing room in which *The Mothman Prophecies* is almost always playing.

According to manager Jeremy Pitchford, odd people sometimes visit the museum late at night. And we're not talking about nerds looking for a cheap thrill. We're talking about the ominous Men in Black, strange men dressed in black suits who are often seen at locations famous for paranormal activity. The Men in Black supposedly gather information on unexplained events for the government (kind of like the movie, but, you know, scarier). Or perhaps the Men in Black are part of the mystery themselves.

According to Pitchford, Wamsley's daughter was working the desk at the museum one night when a man dressed in a black suit came in, asking odd questions.

In 2002, Richard Gere starred in *The Mothman Prophecies*, a low-budget movie that claimed that the Mothman was a spiritual being sent to warn humanity of impending disaster. It was filmed mostly in Pennsylvania.

She wasn't sure the guy was even human. "Do you have any complimentary tobacco or licorice?" he asked her. "You know, years ago, people carried tea with them wherever they went."

If you're interested in a good scare, spend some time at the Mothman Museum in Point Pleasant, but don't stay too late. Be sure to stop in at the Harris Steak House while you're there. And if you find out what Mothman Sauce is, let me know.

Some have noted the similarities between a biblical beast seen in a vision of the apocalypse and the Mothman. Daniel 7:6: "After this I beheld, and lo another, like a leopard, which had upon its back four wings of a fowl; the beast had also four heads; and dominion was given to it."

THE LEGEND OF "RED EYES"

THE EVIL SPIRIT OF CAMP MANATOC

Their first mistake was not paying for a bigger coffin.

But this was the Great Depression and funds were tight, especially for a small Boy Scout camp in northeastern Ohio. You made do with what you had. And what they had was a child-sized coffin and a very tall—and very dead—camp ranger. Don't worry. He died of natural causes: his ticker kicked out during a hike along the perimeter, the way he would have liked to have gone.

Eventually, someone got the idea that what they ought to do is saw off the man's arms, legs, and head in order to make him fit.

To their credit, the camp elders did debate this issue for a short time. It was the camp director who quietly remarked that the ranger had no immediate family, no next of kin, and it was up to them to dispose of his last remains.

And so they drew straws and the man who drew the shortest one, his name lost now to time, was given a handsaw. A trained Eagle Scout, the man made quick work of the flesh. Then they lifted the torso into the coffin and tossed in the arms and legs. But there was no room left for the head. They jumped up and down on the casket, but try as the might, it refused to close.

"What difference does it really make?" asked the camp director.

The head was removed, the coffin was closed, the desecrated body buried on the shores of Lake Litchfield. Unfortunately, there is no record as to where the head ultimately ended up. Some say it was buried beside the coffin, near the lake, only to be dug up and carted off by a wolf. Others suggest it was tossed down a latrine—out of sight, out of mind and all. The truth died with the camp elders.

It wasn't a year later, in 1930, that campers began seeing the red eyes in the woods. From a distance, the young boys would first think the eyes were the light of their lanterns reflected off the eyes of a deer or a coon. But as the red eyes approached, they saw that there was no body, only a decomposed head drifting between the trees, as if searching for something. One boy was struck with such fright upon seeing the disembodied head that he never spoke another word in his life.

Over the years, many boys at Camp Manatoc came

face to face with "Red Eyes" as they ventured into the woods at night to gather kindling. Occasionally, a boy on such an errand would never return. Usually, their bodies were never found—only their heads, which had been cut from their torsos.

At least, that's the story I heard as a young Boy Scout at Camp Manatoc, told by an older kid inside the belly of the old pool's furnace room in 1991.

Imagine the terror I experienced later, when, after having returned to my tent, I peered into the woods a few yards away and spotted two red eyes staring back at me with cold malice. I alerted my friends, sure the red eyes would be gone by the time they looked out. But they were still there. Unmoving. Just staring back at us. And then someone dared me. Dared me to run at it.

I'm sure they believed it was just a small animal, a fox maybe, and they weren't really egging me on to confront a body-less demon from hell. Whatever their intention, I accepted the dare, sure I was about to die, but still hoping to impress my older friends.

I charged at the red eyes. I let loose a war cry.

Five feet into the woods, I came upon it—a meter for

The Camp Manatoc Museum is open to the public every Saturday afternoon. Visit the Manatoc administration building for a tour.

an oil derrick, slowly clicking away, two red lights set into its display.

The legend of Red Eyes is still told around campfires at Camp Manatoc to this day. The Boy Scout camp is tucked away inside the Cuyahoga Valley National Park system, near the town of Peninsula. The entrance is through a wooden gate, big enough to keep in Red Eyes, King Kong, and any other creature that may roam the woods. Inscribed upon the gate, readable only as you leave, is this warning: "To These Things You Must Return."

Bob Hubbard is a legend himself here. The retired Goodyear engineer volunteers his weekends to keep an eye on the young Boy Scouts. The "paychecks started to get in the way of scouting," he says. He tells his own version of the legend to naïve Tenderfoots.

"The story I tell is the story I heard as a scout here, in the fall of 1953, the one about the Mad Farmer," he says. "Back then, the camp extended along the valley all the way to a sheep farm. The man who ran the farm was said to be a little strange. It got so that he couldn't stand the noise coming from the boys at camp during

Camp Manatoc opened in 1923. The Boy Scouts were able to buy the 640 acres thanks to loans from the big three local tire companies—Goodyear, B.F. Goodrich, and Firestone, who each chipped in about a third of the $100,000 purchase price.

the night, so he would walk into camp and try to snatch up any boy who happened to sneak outside his cabin. Sometimes you might see him staring in the window at you."

To Hubbard, the tale is more a tool for scoutmasters than anything else, a way to keep boys inside at night. "Scoutmasters don't want to go chasing after kids in the middle of the night. You get a young boy from the city, first time at camp, and these woods seem endless. And quite scary. Knowing the Mad Farmer is out there keeps them inside."

To this day, young scouts still come up to Hubbard and ask if he's heard about this "Mad Farmer" who lives near Camp Manatoc. "I always say, 'Yes,'" he admits. "I tell them I heard he was spotted in camp and that we're trying to track him down, that they should stay inside at night, just to be safe. It's good fun. Like a scoutmaster sending a kid out to find a left-handed smoke-sifter. Keeps them occupied. I got a boy in here not long ago asking for a left-handed smoke-sifter. I told him I just gave out my last one and that he should check at the admin building, see if they still have one left over there. Of course, then they send him somewhere else."

The current director of the Camp Traditions and History Committee, Rick Misanko, recalls a darker version of the old tale. "The one I heard was called 'The Mad Man of Manatoc,'" he says, estimating the origin of this story to be around 1960.

"Where Lake Litchfield is now, there was the Bloody Gulch. And through the Bloody Gulch ran the Burma Trail. Now, the Mad Man of Manatoc was an evil spirit who would pick off any young boy who happened to straggle behind his hiking group as they made their way over the Burma Trail, there. You had to stay with your troop because sometimes kids would get lost there."

His eyes become glassy as he recalls events from long ago . . .

"Something was killing sheep at the farm beside the camp back then," he says. "It was supposedly a wolf. Though, it could have been a bear—we get those, sometimes. Others said it was the Mad Man, this spirit in the woods. Anyway, kids made a point to stay with their group after that."

These tales of a spirit in the woods go far back, much farther than Hubbard, even, to the days of the Indian tribes that traveled quickly through the Gulch between the Cuyahoga and Tuscarawas rivers. There is *something* here. You can feel it in the air, like potential

The "whistling flagpole" is still there, but the hole is gone. When camp staff moved the flagpole to another field a couple years ago, they had to make it shorter. The section with the hole was sawed off like Red Eye's limbs.

energy gathering before a summer storm. It's an area that feels *thin*, as if the fabric of reality were as worn as the Manatoc flag dancing in the twilight breeze, as if it were stretched to the point of transparency, and that sometimes older creatures from the other side can pass through.

There are stories, too, about scouts feeling sensations of weightlessness near Concord Lodge. Sightings of lights in the sky at night. Reports of odd, futuristic vehicles darting along the trails at three in the morning.

At Camp Manatoc, maybe it's best to stay in your cabin after lights-out.

Just in case.

BIGFOOT'S LAIR

SALT FORK STATE PARK IS SASQUATCH CENTRAL

It's bigger than you expect, this preserve of wilderness. Big enough for many secrets. You can feel it, electricity in the air, in the folds of fine mist that drift between the low trees and rolling hills as cool twilight descends and the nocturnal creatures are free to wander again. *There is something here.*

The entrance to Salt Fork State Park is off Route 22 in rural Guernsey County. A road cuts through the park, taking visitors to campgrounds and beaches, horse riding trails and hiking paths, to a golf course and a giant lodge. The road is surrounded by thick forests of hickory and oak that seem to go on forever. Miles and miles of woods, home to deer and muskrat and, some say, a beast covered in hair that walks upright like a man.

The Delaware Indians, who lived here long before

the white man, were said to have negotiated a truce with the creatures. They often left meat outside for the "Wild Ones" that lived among the trees. In exchange, the Sasquatch would not bother them.

Of the two million visitors who come to the park each year, many know nothing of this legend. But at Salt Fork, even the most jaded skeptic might wind up staring down the creature some call Bigfoot.

In 1972, the year the lodge first opened, a woman driving into the park one night witnessed a bipedal "thing" dart across the road in front of her, its hairy body illuminated by the headlights of her car. She was so shaken up that she called the rangers. One took her statement, then jokingly radioed back to the station that the monster was headed in that direction. A short time later, the ranger stationed in front of the radio at the admin building looked up to the window to find a tall, hairy animal staring back at him.

The sightings grew in intensity throughout the '70s. In 1976, fishermen casting lines into the lake near Hosak's Cave reported tales of a hair-covered female, standing at least seven feet tall, that appeared at the water's edge before walking back into the woods.

Don Keating has hunted Bigfoot in Salt Fork for twenty-seven years. He is arguably the most famous Sasquatch tracker in Ohio, and has appeared on *The Today Show* and *Monster Quest*. A quiet, reserved fellow with an intense stare, Keating looks more like a math teacher than a cryptozoologist. In reality, he works for the county, serving meals to senior citizens in need. Each year, he organizes the Ohio Bigfoot Conference, which is held at the Salt Fork Lodge in May, and draws about 400 believers to the area to trade unbelievable stories about their own encounters.

It was an encounter with a UFO that first caused Keating to question how much we really know about the universe we inhabit. He was thirteen years old in 1976, when his family spotted a bright object in the sky that followed their car down the back roads outside Newcomerstown. "You remember the Jupiter 2 from *Lost in Space*? It looked exactly like that," claims Keating, recalling the incident years later.

The craft followed them all the way to his grandparents' mobile home and hovered, silently just above the treetops as his aunts and uncles came outside to see it for themselves. Then it vanished before their eyes.

"We didn't see it leave like you see an airplane leave

To this day, a film taken in the woods near Bluff Creek, California, in 1967 remains the best evidence for the existence of Bigfoot. Taken by Roger Patterson and Robert Gimlin, the film appears to show a Sasquatch walking quickly away from them and disappearing into the woods. Gimlin is a frequent speaker at the annual Ohio Bigfoot Conference at Salt Fork State Park.

a runway. It was just gone. Here one second, then gone."

During a trip to the library in 1984, on a mission to find information on similar eyewitness accounts of flying saucers, Keating happened upon Bigfoot. It was in a book titled, *Sasquatch: The Apes Among Us*, by John Green.

Ever since, Keating has searched for proof of the creature's existence, concentrating his efforts within the boundaries of Salt Fork, an area he considers to be a hot spot for Bigfoot activity. He does not underestimate the ramifications of such a discovery. "It would be the greatest anthropological find in human history," he says.

For all his searching, though, Keating says he's only gotten one good look at the monster, and it wasn't in Salt Fork.

Due to his notoriety, Keating is often contacted by people who claim to have seen Bigfoot. One such contact came in September 1985, from a man living in Newcomerstown. Keating and three other re-

During Keating's 2009 Bigfoot Conference, a filmmaker from New Zealand punked the group of believers. Leigh Hart, a Kiwi version of Borat, used actual interviews from the convention in a mockumentary that aired overseas in February 2010.

searchers were invited to stake out the creature in the man's backyard. A member of their group recorded a TV program about Bigfoot in which the sounds of the animal were recreated, then dubbed onto cassettes, which they played over a radio pointed into the woods. Shortly after 10 p.m., something strange paid them a visit.

"This thing comes down the hill," says Keating. "Walking upright. Covered in hair. Light in color. It walked into a field of goldenrod that stood five feet high, but it towered over the weeds. I watched it turn toward the chicken coop. Then something spooked it and it turned and quickly ran back up the hill."

Although he has yet to encounter the creature again, he has seen plenty of evidence—the sound of something in the woods, knocking large sticks together, as if warning him to stay away; strange footprints on the shores of the lake near Hosak's Cave. Keating has taught himself how to pour plaster casts and has collected about a dozen decent specimens over the years. The prints appear to come from a creature with feet more apelike than human.

The sightings in Salt Fork persist to this day, and Keating records them now on his Eastern Ohio Bigfoot Investigation Center Web site.

One frightening experience took place at the isolated Handicap Picnic Area. Around 1 a.m., two fellow researchers were returning to their cars after a fruitless night of searching in October 2008, when some

large animal began throwing rocks at them from behind a patch of rose bushes near the pavilion. Being
the only two humans in the area for several hours, they
knew it had to be something else. Was Bigfoot playing
games with them? The veracity of their sighting was
bolstered by a separate eyewitness account of a large
creature seen walking upright near the same rose
bushes.

As recently as 2009, hairy bipedal creatures have
been spotted near Hosak's Cave. Nancy and Bernie
Snodgrass claim to have shone a flashlight on a Bigfoot
clinging to a tree there, as if it were trying to blend in
with the color of the bark, in an attempt at camouflage.
Some wonder if the animal—or animals—might find
shelter in the cave.

Of course, the skeptics want to know why a dead
Bigfoot has never been found at Salt Fork, if so many
are thought to live there.

"Ask a deer hunter how many complete deer car-
casses they've ever come across," says Keating.
"Mother Nature has a good disposal system. In Africa,

**At the 2008 Bigfoot Conference, a speaker named
M. K. Davis presented evidence he claimed proved
that Patterson and Gimlin took part in a Bigfoot
massacre at Bluff Creek after they captured the
creature on film.**

when an 8,000-pound elephant dies, its carcass disappears within ninety-six hours, devoured or scattered by carnivores. In Ohio, we have deer mice that feed on bone and acidic soil that gets rid of what's left."

For Keating, the search is about more than proving the existence of Bigfoot. It's also about appreciating nature. His stakeouts are as much about taking in the beauty of Salt Fork's 17,229 acres of forest and hanging out with friends over a campfire as it is about capturing a Sasquatch on film or finding a dead one to drag back to society.

"Don't go out there trying to find Bigfoot hiding behind a tree," says Keating. "Go out and enjoy nature. And if you see it, consider yourself lucky."

THE COYNE INCIDENT

FLYING SAUCER VS. HELICOPTER ABOVE MANSFIELD

It was supposed to be a routine flight. Cleveland to Wright-Patterson Air Force Base and back in a Huey for a routine physical. In and out. The sort of flight Air Force pilots Arrigo "Rick" Jezzi and Captain Larry Coyne had made a dozen times before. But nothing about this trip would be routine. The men and the bird they were flying that night would be forever changed by the events about to unfold.

October 18, 1973, roughly 10:30 p.m.: Coyne and Jezzi were at the controls of the Huey, pointed toward Cleveland Hopkins Airport, on their way home. Seated behind them were Sergeants John Healey and Robert Yanacsek. Coyne was a straight-edged military commander, a hard-nosed skeptic of all things extraordinary, with nineteen years of flight experience behind him. In civilian life, Jezzi studied chemistry, Healy was a Cleveland cop, and Yanacsek, an early computer whiz. Perhaps it is due to their respectable and intellectual backgrounds that their encounter that night is still regarded by some as a key piece of evidence for the existence of extraterrestrials.

Yanacsek saw it first.

"The best way I can describe it was it looked like a submarine cruising through water," he says, from his Medina home. It has been nearly forty years since the event and time has done nothing to dull his memory. "I could make out its shape because it blotted out the stars behind it. Oblong, thinner at the ends. Like a torpedo, maybe. It was at least 150 feet long and had a red light in front and a white light in the back. And then it turned toward us."

Coyne saw it too and told Yanacsek, his crew chief, to keep an eye on it.

"My first thought," says Yanacsek, "was that it was some student pilot circling around to land at a nearby airport. But we were lit up that night. He should have seen us. But it looked like he was heading right for us. I thought for sure we were going to be hit."

From his seat on the left side of the helicopter, Jezzi's view was blocked by part of the fuselage. But he could hear Coyne's and Yanacsek's conversation growing more and more panicked as the object accelerated toward them. Suddenly, Coyne took control of the Huey, reducing pitch and throwing the bird into auto rotation, a free fall. The chopper plummeted from 2,500 feet to 1,700 before Coyne leveled her out.

The crew looked above them, through the glass dome of the cockpit.

"It hovered above us," says Yanacsek. "It was so close I could see our lights reflecting off its surface, which was grey and textured, but plain. There was no antenna, no wingtips, nothing like that, as far as I could see. It was like a big black submarine was hovering above us."

"It was cigar-shaped," recalls Jezzi, who now lives in western Pennsylvania. "I remember this intense light. Like a spotlight. It was a green light, but that's because it was coming through the Plexiglas window, which was tinted green."

"It hovered over top of us for what seemed like thirty seconds," says Yanacsek. "It was under some kind of control, as if whoever was flying it wanted to take a look at us."

And then, as suddenly as it had appeared, it darted toward the horizon at a high rate of speed and disappeared. When it was gone, Coyne noticed that the he-

Sgt. Arrigo Jezzi went on to work in the R&D labs for such companies as Proctor and Gamble, where he helped develop advanced absorbent material used in modern-day baby diapers.

licopter had inexplicably climbed to 3,500 feet during the encounter.

They called into local airports over the radio. But none had any other aircraft in their vicinity.

After returning to Hopkins, Coyne and his crew filed a report with the FAA and the Army, detailing the strange incident. Soon the media had the scoop. Every paper in town wanted an interview. They were invited to California to re-enact their encounter for a paranormal television show hosted by Rod Serling. Coyne even went on Johnny Carson.

Later, Jezzi traveled to Chicago to meet with Dr. J. Allen Hynek, who had once served as the civilian scientific consultant on the United States government's official UFO investigative unit, Project Blue Book—which, perhaps not coincidentally, had been headquartered at Wright-Patterson Air Force Base. Hynek had been brought in by the Air Force to debunk flying saucer sightings but ultimately became a believer after reviewing a few encounters that defied explanation. Hynek interviewed Jezzi for more than four hours inside the VIP lounge at the O'Hare Airport for a detailed

The military continues to experiment with non-lethal weapons at Wright-Pat, recently helping to develop a microwave beam that can disperse crowds at a distance by quickly heating up the skin of rioters.

report for his newly founded Center for UFO Studies (CUFOS). A detailed summary of that report, written by Jennie Zeidman, a researcher with CUFOS, can be found online.

The "Coyne Incident" as it came to be known, was witnessed from the ground, as well. According to the CUFOS report, a family in a car below, traveling east down Route 430near the Charles Mill Resevoir, saw something "as big as a school bus" engage the helicopter in the night sky. They claimed the light coming from the craft was, indeed, greenish. "It was like rays coming down. The helicopter, the trees, the road, the car—everything turned green."

Coyne and Healey have since passed away, but Yanacsek and Jezzi still reluctantly talk about the encounter whenever a reporter manages to track them down. Although they are at a loss to explain it, neither man has become a fervent believer in little green men.

"I think about it a lot," says Jezzi. "I really don't know what it was. I'm not against believing in UFOs, but was that one? Really? I have no idea."

"Logic would dictate that the craft was terrestrial," says Yanacsek. "But those red and green lights don't make any sense with any traditional aircraft's configuration. I'd give anything just to see it for five seconds in broad daylight so I could know for sure."

Still, there is one piece of evidence that suggests something beyond human understanding took place in the skies over Mansfield that long-ago night. Army engineers thoroughly inspected the Huey after the incident. They discovered that the helicopter's magnetic compass was no longer calibrated correctly. Try as they might, no one could get it to work properly again.

It is interesting to note in passing that part of the medical evaluation the men were given at Wright-Patterson prior to the encounter included a psychological component. Wright-Pat was known to be the headquarters for the military's investigations into reports of flying saucers—some even believe that parts of an alien vehicle that allegedly crashed in Roswell, New Mexico, were shipped to hangar 18 there. Is it mere coincidence that Coyne and his crew were returning from Wright-Pat when they encountered the UFO? Was the saucer some experimental military craft? Were they the subject of a psychological warfare experiment conducted by the Air Force?

On the surface, this would seem like another crazy conspiracy theory. Except, we now know that thirty years ago, scientists at Wright-Pat were developing elaborate non-lethal psychological weapons for war, including "gay bombs" that created homosexual lust among enemy troops and hormones that could be

The National Enquirer awarded Coyne's helicopter crew its blue ribbon award in 1973 for authoring "the most scientifically valuable report" of the year.

sprayed to attract killer bees. They also proposed injecting soldiers with LSD to trigger hallucinations.

But mass hallucination seems unlikely, given the similar testimony collected from witnesses on the ground. There is no question: something strange happened on the way back to Cleveland on October 18, 1973. And both Jezzi and Yanacsek consider themselves lucky to have survived it.

RESURRECT DEAD ON PLANET JUPITER!

WHO CREATED THE TOYNBEE TILES AND WHAT DID THEY WANT WITH OHIO?

The message appeared over time. It was slowly uncovered by the wear and tear of a thousand cars digging into the hot Cleveland pavement. Eventually, the entire colorful tile was revealed at the intersection of Prospect Avenue and West 3rd Street, just past Tower City. It seemed like a warning. This is what it said:

TOYNBEE IDEA
IN MOVIE'2001
RESURRECT DEAD
ON PLANET JUPITER

There was more. In the upper left corner, this was written:

I'M ONLY ONE MAN AND WHEN
I CAUGHT A FATAL DISEASE
THEY GLOATED OVER ITS DEATH

And in small print at the bottom right:

THAT'S WHEN I BEGGED
THEM NOT TO DESTROY IT
THANK YOU AND GOODBYE

Three similar tiles appeared in Cincinnati, along Walnut Avenue. Each, like the one in Cleveland, spoke of a grim plan to populate the largest planet in our solar system with the souls of our dead.

It is difficult to determine when these tiles appeared, due to the nature of their unique design. How long were they under the pavement before being uncovered? Months? Years? We only know that people started to photograph them in Ohio around 2006.

Were the tiles the work of some diabolical mind warning us of his plan to harvest our souls in order to populate the outer planets? Were they the rantings of a crazy person? Perhaps a *dangerous* crazy person? Or were the tiles a work of art—some avant-garde masterpiece? How, exactly, were they even made?

Whatever was happening, the tiles, we discovered, were not limited to Ohio. Similar tiles had been found in cities across the country as far back as the early '80s—there have even been reports of tiles found in

South America, too. But the vast majority of the tiles were concentrated in Philadelphia, a sign, some believed, that the artist lived there.

While the "idea" to resurrect the dead on Jupiter was the main theme, other tiles spoke of a grand conspiracy of societal oppression administered by newspaperman John S. Knight (who owned the Akron *Beacon Journal*), in collusion with the federal government, the USSR, and "the Jews."

Slowly, Toynbee tile researchers began to make sense of the weird messages.

Arnold J. Toynbee, they learned, was a popular British historian who studied the rise and fall of civilizations until his death in 1975. A passage from Toynbee's book, *Experiences*, seems to form the crux of the tiler's plan:

"Human nature presents human minds with a puzzle which they have not yet solved and may never succeed in solving, for all that we can tell. The dichotomy of a human being into 'soul' and 'body' is not a datum of experience. No one has ever been, or ever met, a living

The largest Toynbee tile message was found on four tiles placed together in Philadelphia. It suggested the tiler may have moved. "I secured house with blast doors and fled the country in June 1991," it said. Tiles were found shortly thereafter in Buenos Aires.

human soul without a body ... Someone who accepts— as I myself do, taking it on trust—the present-day scientific account of the Universe may find it impossible to believe that a living creature, once dead, can come to life again."

Several science fiction writers, including Arthur C. Clarke and Ray Bradbury, used Toynbee's philosophies on civilization as background for their novels.

There may also be a connection between the Toynbee tiles and an obscure play by David Mamet. *4 A.M.* is the story of a Larry King-like radio talk show host who is forced to listen to a crazy caller who explains how to reconstitute life on Jupiter. Mamet wrote the play in 1983. It was performed in Philadelphia. Mamet has said he believes the tiles are an homage to his play. Only problem is, some tiles predate Mamet's play—the first verified tiles were discovered in February 1980.

Researcher Justin Duerr, a Philadelphia musician who plays in a variety of popular regional bands such as Northern Liberties and One Rat Brain, may have uncovered another layer to the mystery: the true inspiration of Mamet's play.

According to Duerr, the tiler called the real Larry King in 1980. The recording of the interview, in which a caller freaks out the talk show host with his theory of resurrecting the dead on Jupiter, still exists somewhere in the archives. "I think Mamet heard the broadcast and filed it away in his subconscious," says Duerr. "That's the only explanation that makes sense to me."

Duerr directed a feature-length documentary about the Toynbee Tile mystery that premiered at the Sundance Film Festival. He's spent so much time on the project now, he believes he understands what the tiler was thinking.

"I think one day he had this epiphany," explains Duerr. "Science at that time was revealing some wild things. Scientists were growing human organs on rats. Growing parts of humans outside the body. Maybe he sees *2001* about that same time. Toynbee's ideas on the future of civilization certainly inspired that movie. Then his mind connects these thoughts. He has this idea, a way to show humanity a way to reach a new level of evolution, just like the Star Child at the end of *2001*. He tries to talk about it on *Larry King*. He reaches out to the newspapers, but they think he's a quack. But he thinks this idea is really important and must be shared with everyone. So he starts to think: How do I get my message out there and get it noticed?"

No doubt about it: whoever created these tiles succeeded in getting his message out. But how, exactly, did he do it? Duerr has the answer to that puzzle, too. He claims a freshly dropped tile was once found by a city

The theme of Ray Bradbury's short story, "The Toynbee Convector," is about how humanity can survive by reaching for impossible goals.

worker. It was a plate of linoleum wrapped in tarpaper and simply laid in the street at night. The pressure of car tires would push the tile into the pavement and eventually the paper wrapper would wear off, revealing the message beneath.

"I've made my own," says Duerr, ominously.

But who made the originals? Who was the man who called Larry King and inspired David Mamet? Theories abound on the Internet.

Some point to Hans Heckman, a Philadelphia inventor who experimented with a "spiricom" with two other scientists in the '70s. A spiricom was a device they claimed could be used as a radio to communicate with the dead. One of Heckman's partners claimed to have had 20 hours of conversations with Dr. George Mueller, a physicist who had been dead for several years.

The most popular suspect is James Morasco, a carpenter from Philadelphia who allegedly approached newspapers in the '80s with tales of conspiracies that are referenced in the Toynbee tiles. He died in 2003, and his widow adamantly says he had nothing to do with it.

Directions for making your very own Toynbee tile can be found at ResurrectDead.com. Don't get caught!

Duerr suggests it was Philly recluse Severino Verna, who placed the tiles on the street through a hole in the bottom of his car.

Another theory is that it's Duerr himself, although he would have started placing them when he was four years old, which would make him quite the artist prodigy.

Whoever was responsible for the Toynbee tiles figured Ohioans like us were important enough to include in his great plan. And for that, we thank him. See you on Jupiter!

THE WOW SIGNAL

DID ALIENS REALLY CONTACT AN OHIO STATE UNIVERSITY PROFESSOR IN 1977?

The box arrived on the doorstep of his house that day in August, 1977, full of possibilities. Every few days a technician from Ohio State University left a similar box on his doorstep. It was routine. Box arrives; open the box; pore over its contents; repeat. It had been like this for some time.

Dr. Jerry Ehman took the box inside. He opened it, pulled out the contents: pages of paper spat out by an IBM 1130 computer. Printed on the pages were random groups of numbers, mostly 1s and 2s that meant nothing to the untrained eye. But to Dr. Ehman, the numbers meant everything. The numbers were his life. He was looking for a pattern. And until that day, the pattern had eluded him.

And then he saw it.

On a page dated August 15, he noticed a strange sequence of numbers and letters near the left-hand margin: 6EQUJ5.

The scientist was so excited, he wrote "WOW!" next to it.

6EQUJ5. A meaningless jumble of symbols to most of us.

Only Dr. Ehman and a few of his colleagues knew what the symbols must mean: a signal from a race of intelligent beings outside our solar system.

*   *   *

Dr. Ehman is an appropriate emissary for planet Earth.

He was born on a dairy farm on the outskirts of Buffalo, an only child whose father died early, whose mother was forced to manage the business in his absence until it became too much and they were forced to sell. Mother and son stuck together. After Ehman graduated from high school, she moved with him to a house across the street from the university so he could walk to school.

Ehman was a brainiac, a young man in love with calculations, with physics. In 1960, at the age of twenty, he happened upon an article in *Reader's Digest* about an astronomer named Frank Drake, at Cornell, who was using a radio telescope to listen for signs of intelligent life in outer space. Drake's experiment was dubbed "Project OZMA," after the fictional land of OZ. Drake was using a telescope at the National Radio Astronomy Observatory in Green Bank, West Virginia, to listen to a radio frequency in range of interstellar hydrogen, a frequency that would surely be known to any intelligent extraterrestrial race. Shortly thereafter, Ehman began searching for a grad school with access to a radio telescope.

Initially, Ehman chose the University of Michigan, where he became a research assistant. In 1967, he was courted away by Dr. John Kraus, of OSU, who had constructed a giant radio telescope called "The Big Ear" on land owned by Ohio Wesleyan University in Delaware. Since 1965, Kraus had been using The Big Ear to listen for signals of alien life. He wanted Ehman to help him.

Using The Big Ear, the team at OSU mapped more than 20,000 radio sources in the sky—planets, stars, satellites—and slowly built a map of the known universe. But everything they picked up appeared in the wide-band spectrum of radio waves, a sign that what they were listening to was natural background noise. What they wanted to find were narrow-band signals. The narrower the signal, the more likely it was gener-

Astronomer Frank Drake named his search for E.T.s "Project OZMA", after L. Frank Baum's "OZ", because Baum claimed to have gotten the idea for Dorothy Gale's adventures there by communicating with OZ inhabitants via radio.

ated by intelligent beings. For instance, TV broadcasts and AM radio are narrow-band signals that contain a lot of information.

What the telescope heard was expressed in numbers by the computer. It worked like this: The Big Ear, being fixed to the Earth, carved a path across the sky as the planet rotated. If The Big Ear passed over a star or planet or some source like a satellite that generates its own radio signal, the sound would be expressed as higher and higher numbers on the computer printout. A distant star might register first as a "1," then a "2," then as a "1" again as the star passed through the field captured by the telescope. The higher the number, the narrower the band. If the source became too powerful to be expressed by a single number, the computer switched to letters, A-Z. The team got excited on the rare occasions that the telescope registered a signal stronger than 4 or 5.

In 1972, Congress cut funding and Ehman was out of a job. He landed at Franklin University in Columbus as an adjunct professor teaching business calculus

The IBM 1130 computer that detected the Wow Signal had sixty-four kilobytes of RAM and only one megabyte of memory that had to be reset every three to four days. The "disk" used to store their data was about thirteen inches long.

and other math courses. OSU could no longer afford to staff the telescope, so Ehman volunteered some of his free time at The Big Ear. Fellow astronomer Bob Dixon and Ehman devised rudimentary software so that the telescope could automatically search the sky when no one was around. On "autopilot," the only staff The Big Ear needed was a lab technician who would drop by every three of four days to rip off the printed data. The pages were then packed in a box and dropped off at Ehman's home.

Years. Years of searching. It would seem a daunting and frustrating exploration for anyone who does not appreciate the math behind it that allows for hope.

"Our star is one of about 300 billion in our own galaxy," explains Dr. Ehman, who still lives in Columbus. "Our galaxy is one of about 300 billion other galaxies. To be the only planet with intelligent life among all these stars seems statistically unreasonable."

So they kept looking.

And, on August 15, 1977, Ehman found his signal: 6EQUJ5.

The signal was narrow-band. It was powerful—thirty times more powerful than background noise. And it contained a lot of information.

The first thing Ehman and The Big Ear team did was compare the position of the sound to any known object. But they found no planet, no high-flying plane, no satellite. The signal appeared to have come from deep space, somewhere in the vicinity of a group of stars known as Chi Sagittarii, some 220 light years from Earth.

"It has all the earmarks of a signal from an extraterrestrial civilization," says Ehman. "It may have come from a planet outside our solar system that is so far away it is too dim for us to see."

Like all good scientists, they tried to find it again. In the years since, and as recently as 1996, other astronomers have trained their telescopes to the same region of sky, in hope of hearing Ehman's Wow Signal again. All to no avail. For now, the aliens have grown quiet once more.

Ehman suggests whatever was emitting the signal may have been an instrument used to project the information to random points of space. Think of it as an alien message broadcast from a dish that randomly scans their sky in hope that their message reaches some intelligent being on a distant planet they can't see. Perhaps they are looking for us, too. Perhaps that beam will be directed at our planet again one day.

On September 16, 1994, the second-season premiere of *The X-Files*, titled "Little Green Men," broadcast to TV sets across the United States. Ehman was not listening. If he had tuned in, he would have heard Fox Mulder mention his discovery at The Big Ear observatory.

Still, don't hope for a visit. Though Ehman believes in the existence of many other intelligent beings, the distances involved in space travel prohibit a face-to-face encounter or even a long-distance conversation. If the Wow Signal indeed came from a planet circling a star from Chi Sagittarii, it must have been broadcast 220 years ago. Any reply from us would take another 220 years to reach them. And it would take millennia to travel the distance from here to there, using the most advanced technology we have at our disposal.

The Big Ear was leveled in 1997 to make room for a golf course.

These days, Ehman is actively involved in his church and spends his free time bowling with friends. He is currently going back to school at the age of 70—to get his HAM radio license in an apparent attempt to listen for signals of intelligent life here on Earth.

GOODNIGHT, GRACIE

THE ANGRY GHOSTS OF HOWER HOUSE HATE MEN

The first thing you should know is that the home was built by a reaper.

His name was John Henry Hower, and his company harvested local grain and turned it into cereal, lots and lots of cereal. Enough cereal to make him rich. And he needed a house to go with his wealth.

Hower House was completed in 1871. It sits at 60 Fir Hill, where it casts a long shadow over Akron University and the young female students who are invited inside. As the brochure will tell you, the house is a Victorian mansion, constructed in the Second Empire Italianate style, with twenty-eight rooms full of treasures from around the world. The brochure, handed to visitors as they arrive for the $6 tour, does not mention ghosts. Tour guides laugh off any questions having to do with the paranormal. "Not here," they say.

If you want the real story, you must talk to one of the two young women who live there year-round.

The Hower House was willed to the University of Akron in 1973 by Grace Hower, the matriarch of the family—a woman whose travels and adventures took her to odd corners of the planet, including the tombs of ancient Egyptian pharaohs. The large house requires constant upkeep. And so, in exchange for free lodging and a small stipend, two female students live at Hower House each year in the servants' quarters upstairs. Always two. They keep it clean during the week for fundraisers and tours.

Ashley lived in the Hower House for two years, beginning in 1998. Her sorority sister had invited her to become a caretaker there after another coed left, quickly. When she moved in, she asked the director of the nonprofit organization that raises money for the preservation of the house if it might be haunted.

"She told me, 'No, no, no,'" says Ashley, recalling that first day with a shiver. "But I learned the truth pretty soon. Everyone who has spent time in that house knows it's haunted. But the director doesn't want that reputation."

The first year Ashley was there, things were pretty quiet. There were sounds—footsteps on the hardwood floor, the tinkling of piano keys—but nothing that couldn't be explained away by mice or a strong draft. It wasn't until she moved into the bedroom at the top of the stairs that things took a turn for the worse.

"At night, I started hearing something knocking on my closet door—from the inside," says Ashley. "And then I noticed the closet door had a lock on the outside. Why would you put a lock on a closet door?"

To keep something—or someone—in, of course.

Ashley asked some of the volunteers who lead the tours about it. She was told that a century ago, a servant used to lock her kids in the closet when they were bad. After that, Ashley slept with the closet door open.

One afternoon, while exploring the library, Ashley discovered two binders hidden behind a row of old books. One was full of happy events, clipped from the *Beacon Journal*: weddings, births, awards. The other was full of tragedies: obituaries, fatal accidents, natural catastrophes. What sort of person would want to collect such things?

When another young woman moved in, a feeling of dark gloom quickly settled over the house and its inhabitants. Something had changed. Ashley and her

One popular story among Hower House residents is of a school security guard who was called to check out a disturbance late one night. He left his shoes at the door so he wouldn't dirty the floors. While walking the halls he claimed he heard a female voice say, "Get out of my house!" He was so frightened, he ran out of the house, leaving his shoes behind.

roommate would sit at the stairs at night and listen to the piano playing in the parlor. They heard someone rustling the clothes hangers in the closet at the foot of the stairs. And the knocking from inside the closet grew louder, more urgent.

KNOCK KNOCK KNOCK KNOCK

Let me ouuuuuut!

One night, the noises were so loud they called the police. The responding officer refused to come inside until reinforcements arrived. "Bring your proton packs," he jokingly called into the radio.

As the cops searched the house, one told Ashley that she wasn't the first to call them over. The disturbances, he said, go back for decades. On the way out, one officer was convinced that the eyes of the woman on the large picture by the front door were following his every move.

"That was Grace," says Ashley. "Grace's picture."

Only a few weeks later, Ashley saw Grace again.

In a 1997 *Beacon Journal* interview, the Hower House director admitted a former resident used to lock her brother in the closet of the servant's room. One day, the boy was locked inside with a hammer (a handy tool to keep with you if you think you might be locked in a closet). The marks made by the boy's furious hammering can still be seen in the door.

Only this time, she was no longer confined to the photograph.

"I was sitting in my room with my boyfriend," she recalls. "He was sitting on the floor, facing the bedroom door, which has these glass windows that look out into the hallway. I was talking to him and all of a sudden, his face froze, and I saw an old woman walk by in a nightgown. When this person went by, you couldn't hear any footsteps."

Ashley eventually learned that there was a reason only women were asked to become caretakers of Hower House.

"I called my old roommate, the one who gave me the job, and she told me that Grace didn't like men in the house," says Ashley.

The night her roommate brought a male friend upstairs, Ashley awoke to find every candle in her room lit, even though she only kept them there for decoration. "I felt like I was going crazy."

The final straw was when something went after her boyfriend. "He woke me up one night and he was covered in sweat," she says. "He said one of the sheets had wrapped around his neck. He felt like something was trying to choke him. And he heard a female voice whispering something horrible in his ear.

Ashley left soon after. And another young woman took her place.

It was around this time that a reporter with the university's student newspaper, *The Buchtelite*, made a startling discovering in the archives in the basement of Polk Hall. There, he discovered a letter written by John Henry Hower to his son, Milton, in the year 1900. "In regard to the strange lights that John B., you, and Blanche saw," it reads, "they may have been of a similar kind that your mother used to see when she lived in the house. A light would appear in her bedroom, but strangely, no one could see it but herself. How very slightly it appeared and not now. But the last time it appeared was, I think, the first night we slept together. It used to worry her, but apparently it had no significance of evil."

*   *   *

A recent trip to the Hower House found a Victorian exhibition in full swing, the house packed with visitors.

When asked about the ghosts, assistant director Linda Bussey is quick to dismiss. "There are no ghosts here," she says. "Who told you that?"

But when she walked away, a young woman in the

> **Another explanation for the increase in strange activity whenever men visit the house may be the broken promise of John Hower himself, who told his first wife, Susan, that he would never be with another woman if she were to die. Four years after her untimely demise, he remarried.**

corner took my hand like some childhood conspirator and led me upstairs. The walls on the second floor are decorated with battalion maps from the Civil War, the bedrooms stuffed with furniture spirited away from South American countries where the Howers once owned grapefruit plantations. A display of rusty weapons lines one landing. The house is lousy with black walnut. We stopped in front of the servants' quarters.

"I'm not going to take you inside," she whispered. "But that's my bedroom. And there's something in the closet! I can hear it at night. We're told not to talk about it."

The young woman said she has also seen a little girl running around the halls.

"What does she look like?"

Just then, the assistant director returned and asked the young woman to tend to the guests downstairs.

"It was the girl in the big painting in that other room," she said as she left, pointing at a bedroom at the other end of the hall.

Inside the bedroom is an ornate mirror, and, above a mantel, a painting of a beautiful young girl with long dark hair.

"Who is that?" I asked a volunteer standing nearby.

"The young girl in the painting? That's the last owner of the house. That's Grace."

DR. KROH'S HOME FOR PECULIAR CHILDREN

THE MELON HEADS OF KIRTLAND CRAVE REVENGE . . . AND YOUR BLOOD!

There is something wrong with Kirtland. It's a sense of otherness, as if this picturesque land of rolling hills and thick forests exists in one of those "thin" places you read about in old Lovecraft stories, a place where reality has worn so thin, creatures from the other side might crawl through. You feel it in your bones, in the way the hairs stand up on your arms, a deep feeling of wrongness that persists. It has been like this as far back as anyone can remember.

From 1831 to 1838, Kirtland was the headquarters of the Church of Latter Day Saints. The so-called prophet, Joseph Smith, brought his followers here. According to LDS legend, those who attended the church's dedication ceremony witnessed other-worldly beings and lesser gods gathering around the steeple.

The stringent rules of the universe seem . . . *wonky* in Kirtland. People who visit Gravity Hill on King Memorial Road claim that when they put their cars in neutral there, the vehicles will roll uphill.

There is no doubt that Kirtland is cursed. This is, after all, where Jeffrey Lundgren killed five people in 1989. Lundgren worked as a tour guide at the Kirtland Temple, now home to a splinter group of the Latter Day Saints. After church elders accused him of theft and fired him, Lundgren moved to an old farmhouse on Chardon Road and began preaching "the truth" to a growing cult of his own. On April 17, 1989, Lundgren and his followers "pruned the vineyard" by sacrificing five of their own, an entire family: two adults, three kids. Lundgren was trying to bring about the end of the world. He only succeeded in bringing about the end of his own—he was executed for the Avery family murders in 2006.

So it's not surprising that such a place would give rise to another story of human depravity and cold-blooded revenge: the legend of the Melon Heads.

*   *   *

There is little documentation to rely on, but the oft-agreed-upon specifics are as follows: shortly after World War II, a physician known as "Dr. Kroh" and his wife settled into a large estate on Wisner Road in Kirtland. Kroh was a self-described "geneticist" who studied the writings of one Gregor Mendel, a nineteenth-century scientist who created strange hybrids in the lab. Kroh's wife was more of a classic philanthropist, and devoted much of her time to children's charities.

Mrs. Kroh began to adopt children . . . and, at night, Dr. Kroh began to experiment on them.

The serums he injected into the kids had an unexpected side effect: it altered the size of their brains, making their heads grow to odd proportions. When Mrs. Kroh finally uncovered the truth, she threatened to leave him. Dr. Kroh grew incensed and pushed her against a wall, hard enough to knock her unconscious. Seeing this, the large-headed children attacked Dr. Kroh. In the struggle, a lamp was knocked over, and soon the entire house was engulfed in flames.

Investigators believed everyone had perished in the fire, as there were skeletons with giant skulls among the ruins, kneeling beside the remains of Mrs. Kroh. Except that the local authorities did not know how

Wisner Road is also home to a "crybaby bridge." Near Kroh's supposed estate, a small bridge spans a tributary of the Cuyahoga. Locals say a distraught woman threw her baby off the bridge a hundred years ago. If you park your car on the bridge at midnight, you can hear it crying from below.

many children the Krohs had cared for, and all records of adoption were destroyed in the blaze.

Soon after, people driving along Wisner Road began to report strange creatures running after their cars or trailing them through the woods. The monsters were the size of tall children, but had gigantic heads and dark, beady eyes. Sometimes these beings grew bold enough to steal chickens from neighboring farms. One was spotted devouring a family dog, still tied to its backyard leash.

To this day, the reports continue. And some wonder if the drugs Dr. Kroh used on them might have also made the children immortal.

*   *   *

An investigation into the Melon Head attacks suggests a nugget of truth to this legend. The people who live on Wisner Road today are quite familiar with the story, but the only thing they're really afraid of are the carloads of obnoxious teens who speed down the road on Halloween, hoping to catch a glimpse of the monsters. The truth, they say, is not so frightening.

There are also reported sightings of Melon Heads in Laketown, Michigan, and Fairfield County, Connecticut. Both regions once had asylums that treated hydrocephalic children.

It seems a doctor did live on Wisner Road after World War II. He had a child with hydrocephalus, a condition that causes excess water to accumulate around the brain, making the child's skull grow to abnormal size. The child used to play along the road and would occasionally startle those who drove by.

Or maybe there were two children with deformities. Nobody can really remember that far back.

"There was this doctor who lived here, who had some mongoloid children," says Nancy Gorman, who runs a horse stable on Wisner Road. "People were just scared of them because they didn't know better."

Genetic anomaly or genetic experiment? Which one would you rather face in the dark, cursed woods of Kirtland?

Some have noted how the descriptions of the Kirtland Melon Heads resemble an alien race referred to as "the Greys." Perhaps they are not genetic mutations after all. Perhaps they're visitors from a distant planet of Melon Heads . . .

OHIO'S OLDEST MONSTER

FOR CENTURIES, A SEA SERPENT HAS STALKED THE SHORES OF LAKE ERIE

I was going to skip this one. A giant prehistoric sea serpent living in Lake Erie? Yeah, right. The stories, I figured, had likely been dreamed up in some Huron County bar, over a couple Red Stripes and Jim Beam sidecars. It was a way to generate interest in the area. A clever hoax. Had to be. I doubted there was even anything to really research. Certainly nothing in the way of first-hand testimony or historical record.

I couldn't have been more wrong.

Written accounts of a great aquatic monster in Lake Erie go back *centuries*. Millennia, perhaps, because the Indians who lived here before white men arrived had their own legend about something in the lake that had scales like a fish, slithered like a snake on the surface of the water, but could creep onto land using large flipper-like appendages. I've been made a believer.

There is something in this lake. Probably not a living dinosaur. But *something*. Something huge and mysterious. There are simply too many sightings to disregard. Consider:

*   *   *

A report that appeared in the *Cleveland Register* in 1918: "Not a summer has been passed for more than three years, but that one of the most terrific of all sea monsters ever in existence has been seen in different parts of the lake." That same year, a schooner captain encountered the creature and stated: "The serpent's body was larger than the mast of any ship."

*   *   *

From the May 21, 1892, edition of the *Plain Dealer*: "Lake Erie Sea Serpent: Said to Have Been Seen by Fishermen Near Oak Harbor. It was described to be about twenty-five feet long and about one and one-half feet in diameter through the largest part. Its head was large and flat. About five feet from its head there appeared to be several large fins or flippers. Its color was black, mottled with brown spots. It did not offer to molest the men but swam out into the deep water, where it has not been seen since."

*   *   *

In 1898, according to local published reports, a hunter discovered four abnormally large eggs buried in the sand on the shore of Lake Erie. Believing the eggs were fossils, the man took them home. "He put them in a blanket near the kitchen stove. He forgot about them but when the family went into the kitchen the day following, they were astonished to see four snakes wriggling around the kitchen floor," reported the *Plain Dealer*. "The reptiles were from two and a half to five feet long, though no bigger around than a broom stick. The Fosters have kept one snake, and since last Saturday, when it was hatched, it has grown more than a foot in diameter." The paper confidently concluded: "The west end of Lake Erie is still inhabited by sea serpents of no inconsiderable size."

*   *   *

Another headline, from 1909: "Ware Ye Sailors: Serpent is Here! Wriggly Dragon, Grayish-Green and of Playful Disposition, is Seen in Lake." A group of workers at the Union Salt Company watched something willowy and snakelike churn up water on the surface of the lake for several minutes. "The crowd that had gathered made a rush for a boat owned by the Union Salt works, but before the craft could be launched, the serpent had disappeared beneath the surface and,

Huron Lagoons Marina offers a $100,000 for the safe capture of the beast.

as men are not paid to trail sea serpents, its further course was not discovered. When last observed it was headed straight for Euclid beach."

* * *

Then, in 1931, two men rowed their boat into a Sandusky harbor, claiming they had killed and captured the creature. While on the lake, a great serpent had attacked their boat, they said, and they fought back with their oars, striking the monster dead. "A cloud of a sort of blue-white vapor came up from it," one man told a reporter. The men kept it in a box in a garage and people came from all over to see the carcass—after paying a small fee, of course. And when credible scientists assured people the body was merely that of a dead python, probably someone's stray pet, the lines of suckers only grew longer.

* * *

The sightings died down for some time after that, but then picked up again in the early '80s. The *Port Clinton Beacon*, a weekly newspaper for that region, held a contest to name the monster. One reader suggested

Tom Schofield built a replica of "Lemmy," the lake serpent that stood near the mouth of the Huron River. After he died, his son built another one, this time with red lights for eyes.

"South Bay Besse," a reference to the nearby Davis-Besse nuclear power plant, that some have suggested may have mutated a snake to bizarre proportions. Eventually, South Bay Besse became "Bessie."

*   *   *

A charter boat captain named John Liles told the *Plain Dealer* that he had seen the sea serpent as recently as 1993, between Huron and Maumee Bay. "I know what I saw," said Liles. "The thing is huge. I didn't see the head, just the tail flopping in the water toward the end of it."

Unless you want to discount these numerous accounts, going back centuries, you must believe that there is something swimming around Lake Erie. Something huge.

Some biologists have theorized that Bessie might be a 300-year-old sturgeon or a giant freshwater eel or just a really big black snake. Whatever it is, even they agree, it must be something unique. And big enough to command our respect.

So if you should chance upon the Lake Erie Monster, steady your oar. Pick up a camera, instead. We'd all like a glimpse of it, too!

In 1913, the *Plain Dealer* asked people to send in accounts of the sea monster, paying submitters up to $8 per article.

WHAT HAPPENS ON RATTLESNAKE ISLAND STAYS ON RATTLESNAKE ISLAND

THE TRUE STORY OF THE MOST ELITE SECRET SOCIETY IN OHIO

What if I told you there was a secret island on Lake Erie where the richest people in Ohio—the one-per-centers of the Buckeye State—gather every summer to bask in the sunshine, far from the prying eyes of journalists and the nosy lower classes? Trust me. It's there. I've seen it. If you've ever climbed the steps to the top of Perry's Monument on South Bass Island, you've seen it, too: that green island in the distance, just beyond Middle Bass, the one that looks kind of like a toddler's toy rattle. If you have powerful binoculars, you might be able to see a couple mansions—and the little hotel—on the island's north side. But unless you have at least $65,000 to burn or know someone who does, you will never set foot there. They call it Rattlesnake Island. And it was once home to bootleggers and mobsters. Today, it's occupied by even more nefarious folk.

For a long time, little was known about the exclusive group that maintains the island beyond the strange rumors overheard in Put-in-Bay bars. Sometimes curious vacationers would drive their boats too close to the docks there, only to be met by men with guns. But who did these guards work for? Who was in charge?

It was only in 2008, when a former employee of Rattlesnake Island came forward, that we finally got a glimpse inside this covert club. The man came to me. And the story he had to tell was even more bizarre than I could have imagined.

*   *   *

His name was Matt Boggs, and for a time he worked as an assistant manager for the Rattlesnake Island Club. Boggs is one of those free spirit types, always looking for adventure, willing to work in odd places for odd people. One summer, he managed St. Hazard's Resort on Middle Bass. He was prepared, mentally, for living on a small island: the isolation, the eccentricities of its residents. So when he heard the Rattlesnake Island Club (or, the RIC, as it's known) was looking for a manager, he applied right away.

He was contacted by RIC operations manager Nastia Pak, a Lithuanian woman, who asked Boggs to meet at a steak house in Independence for an interview. She brought Keith Folk with her. Nobody knows the island like Folk. He's the resident caretaker, and the only person who stays on Rattlesnake year-round. The interview went well, but before they could hire him, Boggs needed to have a sit-down with the president of the RIC, Bob Serpentini.

Yes, *that* Bob Serpentini—the prolific Ohio auto dealer who became locally famous for his "American, and prrrroud of it!" catch phrase. You know, the guy whose name is on the Lakewood ice arena.

Serpentini invited Boggs to Ken Stewart's Lodge in Bath. The car king can often be found at the lodge, sipping vodka or dining at Stewart's Grille in Akron. According to articles that appeared in the *Beacon Journal*, Serpentini first met Stewart at a health club in 1993, and they became fast friends. For a birthday, Stewart even bought Serpentini a pair of cuff links engraved with "K" for "Ken."

When Boggs arrived at Stewart's Lodge, Serpentini was sitting with another RIC member, Gary Taylor, chairman of the board of the telemarketing firm In-

Rattlesnake Island has its own federally sanctioned post office and issues unique triangle stamps.

foCision, who got his start as marketing director for televangelist Rex Humbard. The interview was very brief. Serpentini quizzed Boggs on his résumé and when he was done, simply said, "You can leave now."

Serpentini's brusqueness was disconcerting, but Boggs desperately wanted to know the secrets of the island. Soon he was on a boat headed for the club's private docks, luggage in hand.

Accommodations for the sixty-eight members of the RIC are surprisingly low-key. There's one restaurant on the island, the Golden Pheasant Inn, which has no cash register because everything is billed to members' accounts. In 2008, Chef Terrance Galvin, Nastia's husband, claimed he could "prepare anything to your exact wishes." There is a golf course, but it only has four holes and you have to play through the island's airstrip. The whole time Boggs was there, the hot tub was always broken.

Boggs roomed with the staff of the RIC in the dorms, which were three mobile homes pushed together with a common room in the middle section. The other staff members—waitresses, cleaning crew, bartenders—were almost entirely beautiful young Eastern European women in the states on short-term visas. The

The island once served as a summer retreat for Catholic schoolboys.

women, says Boggs, came from countries like Ukraine and Moldavia, and were hand-selected by RIC members from dossiers that always included photographs. The young women were paid minimum wage and were forced to pool their tips, which were distributed by Nastia. Most didn't make enough to pay the $100 round-trip toll to get to South Bass on their day off. It's a strange utopia for a man like Serpentini, who bills himself as an American patriot.

Also off-putting was the way they got rid of garbage on the island. Boggs says the trash was burned nightly behind the men's dorm. Folk once told him they only carted garbage off the island once a year. It was just too expensive.

And then there was "Jesse," the masseuse. RIC members could call into the island and request a massage from Jesse in the hotel, and she would come in from the mainland for the night. Boggs met the young blonde as she helped herself to drinks behind the bar at the Golden Pheasant one night. Jesse lives in Ohio, but her Web site advertises services "anywhere in the country." Strangely, the Ohio Medical Board, which maintains records on all licensed massotherapists in the state, has no record of her.

Perhaps the strangest thing that happened to Boggs during his brief stay on Rattlesnake Island was when one member offered him $3,000 if he would bring a "Russian" girl to his room. He politely declined.

Boggs was eventually fired after a weird incident

involving the wife of K&D CEO, Doug Price. According to Folk, she claimed that Boggs had been rude to her when she asked him to find her some cigarettes. Back on the mainland, Boggs filed for unemployment. At first, the RIC tried to deny his claim, but eventually relented after the Department of Job and Family Services requested further details of Boggs' dismissal.

Years later, Boggs is still guarded with information, such as the identities of the RIC members. They are the sort of people with deep pockets, not the kind you really want to anger.

However, by searching scant public records in Ottawa County, other members are revealed. A liquor license shows that Victor Arsena is club V.P. Arsena is a local contractor who got in a bit of legal trouble a while back after transferring $765,000 from his employees' retirement plans to benefit himself and his brother. The case was settled when the Arsenas agreed to pay back the money.

Auditor records list the names of the members who own homes on the island. There's Bud Koch, former CEO of Charter One, Cincinnati developer Craig Hilsinger, local businessman Ray Fogg, and contractors

Elizabeth Taylor, Frank Sinatra, and Kid Rock have all reportedly stayed the night on Rattlesnake Island. Probably not together.

William Scala and Nathan Zampelli, whose company built Stewart's Lodge. The ownership of two other lots remains hidden behind limited liability companies using third-party agents.

When asked about the odd activities on Rattlesnake Island, member Frank Ilcin, a partner at Deloitte & Touche, says gruffly, "We're a private island. We're kind of free to do what we want to do."

ABOUT THE AUTHOR

James Renner is a novelist, freelance journalist, and blogger. In his spare time, he hunts serial killers. His true crime stories have been published in the Best American Crime Reporting and Best Creative Nonfiction anthologies. His film adaptation of a Stephen King story was an official selection at the 2005 Montreal World Film Festival. A graduate of Kent State University, Renner lives in Akron, Ohio.

www.jamesrenner.com

OTHER BOOKS OF INTEREST . . .

Strange Tales from Ohio 2nd Edition
True Stories of Remarkable People, Places, and Events in Ohio History

Neil Zurcher

Ohio history can get pretty strange! Meet Ashtabula's famed Headless Chicken, who lived without his noggin for 38 days. Was Ohio really bombed by the Japanese in WWII? Introducing the inventor of disposable diapers . . . For anyone who enjoys history with a twist, here are 75 tales of the Buckeye State's most unusual people, places, and events.

"A delightful read . . . Zurcher chooses his anecdotes well, balancing scandalous murder mysteries and the truly odd with lighter fare about Ohio's famous inventors and funniest first achievements." – Akron Life Magazine

Ohio Oddities 2nd Edition
A Guide to the Curious Attractions of the Buckeye State

Neil Zurcher

The Buckeye State has no shortage of strange, silly, goofy, quirky, eccentric, and just plain weird places, people, and things—if you know where to look. Discover the World's Largest Cuckoo Clock, the nation's only vacuum cleaner museum, Balto the Wonder Dog, the "bottomless" Blue Hole of Casalia, and lots more hard-to-believe stuff!

"Oddly delightful . . . From the Blue Hole to the headless chicken, it's a wonderfully wacky page turner." – Martin Savidge, CNN

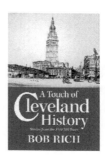

A Touch of Cleveland History
Stories from the First 200 Years

Bob Rich

These 57 short stories are an entertaining introduction to the history of Cleveland, Ohio, for natives or newcomers. They highlight exceptional people and notable events from log cabin days to the mighty industrial era, and cover subjects from sports to fashion to crime. For any Clevelander who wants to know a little more about the old hometown.

Read samples at **www.grayco.com**

OTHER BOOKS OF INTEREST . . .

The Serial Killer's Apprentice
And 12 Other True Stories of Cleveland's Most Intriguing Unsolved Crimes

James Renner

An investigative journalist cracks open 13 of Northeast Ohio's most intriguing unsolved crimes, including the 1964 murder of Garfield Heights teen Beverly Jarosz; the West Side disappearances of Georgina DeJesus and Amanda Berry; the mysterious suicide (or murder?) of Joseph Kupchik; and ten other equally haunting tales.

"James Renner is genuine. He cares about these victims . . . When it comes to true crime, this is the kind of writer we need." – Crime Shadow News

Amy: My Search for Her Killer
Secrets and Suspects in the Unsolved Murder of Amy Mihaljevic

James Renner

A young journalist investigates the cold case that has haunted him since childhood: the 1989 disappearance of 10-year-old Amy Mihaljevic from Bay Village, OH. Filled with mysterious riddles, incredible coincidences, and a cast of odd but very real characters, his investigation quickly becomes a riveting journey in search of the truth.

"Poignant and wonderfully well-written." – Richard North Patterson, New York Times bestselling author of Silent Witness

They Died Crawling
And Other Tales of Cleveland Woe

John Stark Bellamy II

The foulest crimes and worst disasters in Cleveland history are recounted in 15 incredible-but-true tales. Delves into the city's most notorious moments, from the 1916 waterworks collapse to the Cleveland Clinic fire to the sensational Sam Sheppard murder trial. These gripping narratives deliver high drama and dark comedy, heroes and villains.

"A rollicking, no-holds-barred account of the facts (and continued speculation) about some of the darkest events and weirdest people in Cleveland's history." – Youngstown Vindicator

Read samples at **www.grayco.com**